The Rice Bag Hammock

Written by

Shaeeza Haniff

Illustrated by

Swafeha Khan

© 2012 Text Shaeeza Haniff
© 2012 Illustrations Swafeha Khan

All rights reserved. No part of this document may be reproduced or transmitted in any form or by any means, electronic, mechanical, photocopying, recording, or otherwise, without prior written permission of Publisher.

ISBN-13: 978-1461126621

ISBN-10: 1461126622

SherKhan aka Samseer

1906 - 1988

We lovingly dedicate this book to our wonderful Aaja who always had time to make rice bag hammocks.

S.H & S.K

It started as a simple burlap bag that held the rice that Aaja grew.

Wise, nimble, clever hands using a
big curved needle and brown twine
sewed together the
rice bag hammock that Aaja made.

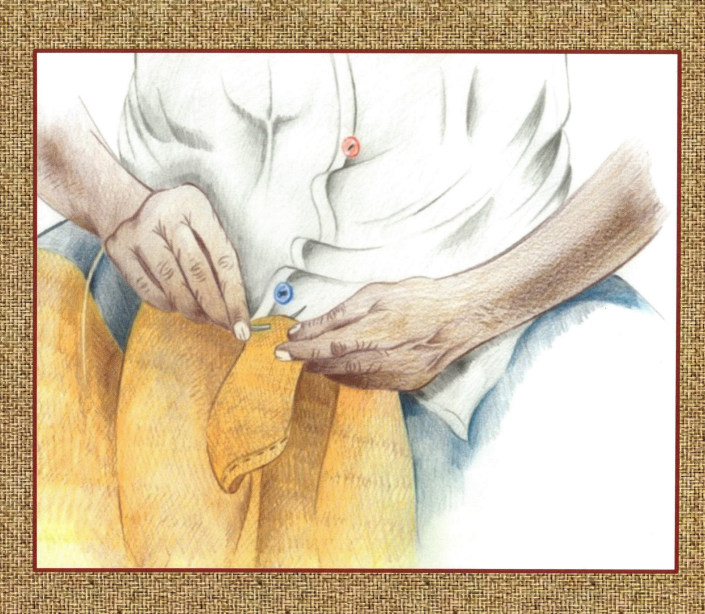

A solemn meeting place for
conversing elders is the
rice bag hammock that Aaja made.

A gentle rocking place for
a sleeping baby is the
rice bag hammock that Aaja made.

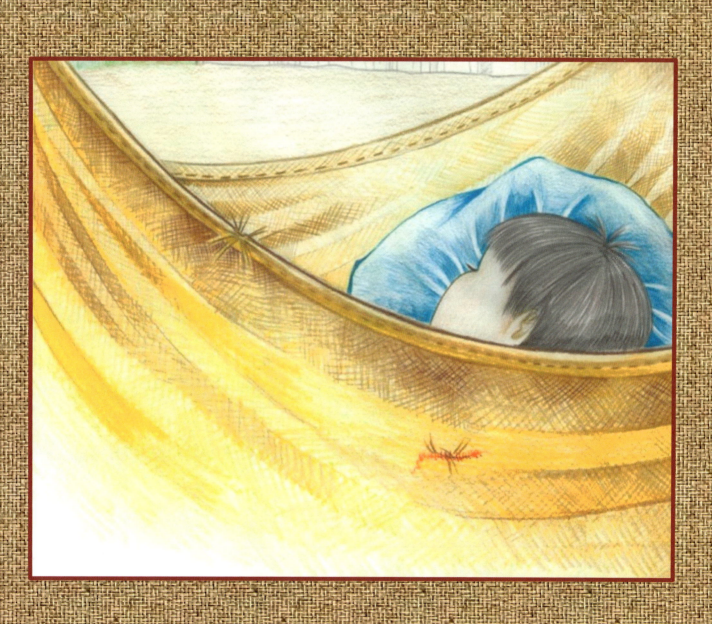

A chatty place for cousins making coconut brooms is the rice bag hammock that Aaja made.

A still, soothing place for
a sick person is the
rice bag hammock that Aaja made.

A friendly place for greeting friends old and new is the rice bag hammock that Aaja made.

A calm place for a
waiting uncle or aunt is the
rice bag hammock that Aaja made.

An imaginative place for
a young reader is the
rice bag hammock that Aaja made.

An "alone time" place for

my thoughts is the

rice bag hammock that Aaja made.

A moonlit planning place for

a young couple is the

rice bag hammock that Aaja made.

A breezy place to get out of
the midday heat is the
rice bag hammock that Aaja made.

A cool resting place for Aaja after the hot rice fields is the rice bag hammock that Aaja made.

A cocoon like place for
hide 'n seeking children is the
rice bag hammock that Aaja made.

A preparation place for
Aajee to use for meals is the
rice bag hammock that Aaja made.

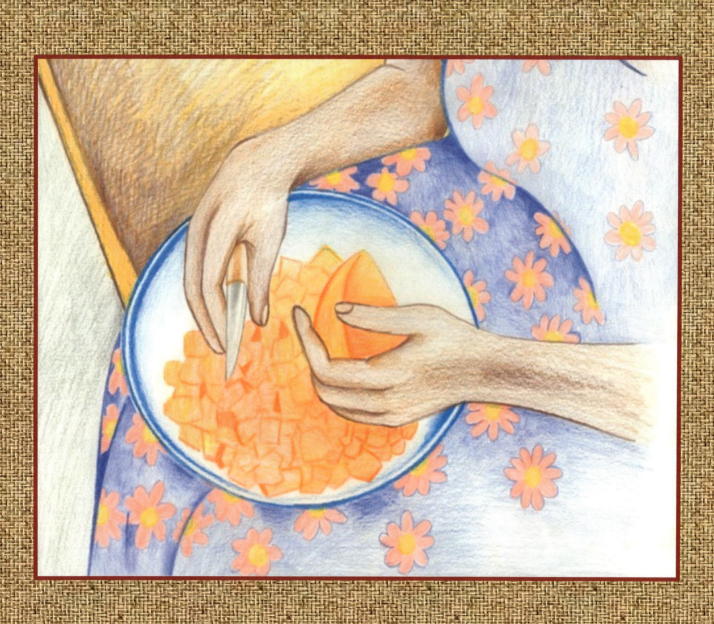

An observation place for curious faces at harvest time is the rice bag hammock that Aaja made.

A high swinging place for
singing cousins is the
rice bag hammock that Aaja made.

Until one day……

KER-PLOP!!!!

"Aaja, it's time to make a rice bag hammock!"

Glossary

Aaja – North Indian word meaning paternal grandfather

Aajee – North Indian word meaning paternal grandmother.

About the Author

First born of the former Chief Education Officer of Guyana and his wife, Shaeeza grew up in the coastal region of tropical Guyana, South America. Her childhood was filled with memories of large family gatherings, dozens of cousins, aunts, uncles and many song filled hammock swings. Aaja was prominent in her life until his death in 1988. Shaeeza along with her two sisters and one brother listened to stories of his many trips abroad filled with adventures and laden with minute detail. His gift for storytelling seems to have passed down to Shaeeza as she has been writing and making up stories since she was ten years old.

She gets inspiration for her books from her family, memories of her childhood and her many students. Many of her stories are based on real events and incidents or conversations.

Shaeeza now lives in Binghamton, New York with her husband, five children and two cats.

This is her first published book.

About the illustrator

Swafeha Khan, an artist living in Coconut Creek, Florida is Shaeeza's youngest sister.

Sharing many of the same experiences as her older sister, Swafeha grew up as an artist, investigating, noticing, sketching, drawing, coloring her days away. She was first inspired to become an artist when as a homework assignment at about age nine she had to draw a bird. Asking her mom for help, she was amazed that her mom could draw and became determined to draw pictures as well as her mom.

She graduated from the Burrowes' School of Art and the University of Guyana with an art degree. She attended a Disney/UNICEF animation workshop hosted by Carimac University of West Indies, Jamaica.

Swafeha continued with her love of art as an art teacher. She worked as a freelance design consultant in Guyana.

She gets her inspiration from nature and from her kids. Among all the mediums for art, her favorite is the paper and pencil as this was what she has been using all her life. The subject that brings her the most joy in drawing and coloring are botanicals and she finds a way to include them in most of her work.

She now lives in Coconut Creek with her husband, four kids and three cats. This is her first illustrated book.